James L. Andem

Temperance in the American Congress

James L. Andem

Temperance in the American Congress

ISBN/EAN: 9783337232559

Printed in Europe, USA, Canada, Australia, Japan

Cover: Foto ©Suzi / pixelio.de

More available books at **www.hansebooks.com**

TEMPERANCE

IN THE

AMERICAN CONGRESS.

ADDRESSES BY

Hon. Schuyler Colfax,	Hon. Hiram Price,
Hon. Henry Wilson,	Hon. Samuel McKee,
Hon. Richard Yates,	Hon. F. E. Woodbridge,
Hon. William E. Dodge,	Hon. J. B. Grinnell,

Hon. J. W. Patterson,

DELIVERED ON THE OCCASION OF THE

First Meeting of the Congressional Temperance Society, Washington, D. C.,

HELD IN THE HOUSE OF REPRESENTATIVES,

February 17th, 1867,

WITH A LIST OF PLEDGED MEMBERS.

REPORTED BY JAMES L. ANDÉM, PHONOGRAPHER.

NEW YORK:

SAMUEL R. WELLS, PUBLISHER,

No. 389 BROADWAY.

1867.

Invitation.

~~~~~~~~~~~~

WASHINGTON, D. C., *February* 13, 1867.

DEAR SIR:

You and your family are respectfully invited to be present at a Congressional Temperance Meeting, to be held in the Hall of the House of Representatives, on Sunday evening, the 17th instant, at seven o'clock, to encourage, by your presence, the effort to stay the progress of the tide of intemperance which is now desolating the land.

The people are looking to Congress to give their powerful influence in aid of an object of such vital interest to our entire country.

If not disposed to unite with the Society, it is most desirable that you give it the influence of your presence.

S. COLFAX,	RICHARD YATES,	} EXECUTIVE COMMITTEE.
S. C. POMEROY,	J. W. PATTERSON,	
W. E. DODGE,		

THE

Congressional Temperance Society.

Long before the hour announced for the opening of the meeting, the spacious galleries of the Representative Chamber were filled to their utmost capacity, in response to the call of the Executive Committee, by citizens of Washington and sojourners from different States and Territories of the Union, and by seven o'clock the reserved seats on the floor of the Hall were all taken by Senators, Representatives, and their families. Hundreds of persons were obliged to turn away, not being able to find even standing-room within sound of the speakers' voices.

Soon after seven o'clock, the meeting was called to order by the Chairman, Hon. HENRY WILSON, of Massachusetts.

Prayer was offered by Rev. Mr. ORCUTT, of New Jersey.

After which the Chairman addressed the meeting as follows:

ADDRESS OF HON. HENRY WILSON,

Of Massachusetts.

LADIES AND GENTLEMEN—Several members of the Senate and House of Representatives, mindful of the measureless evils and sorrows of intemperance, have formed a society, in which we have pledged each to the other, and all to country and to God, to put from us forever the fatal cup of intoxication. [Applause.] On this holy Sabbath evening the Society has summoned members of Congress, temperance organizations, and the people of the national capital, to meet in this chamber of the representatives of the people, publicly to commit ourselves, to the full extent of all we are and all we hope to be, to the hallowed cause of Temperance. In the name of the Society, I bid welcome here to-night to these members of Congress, these societies, and this people that crowd this chamber and throng these galleries. I bid you, one and all, welcome on this occasion, which we humbly trust, in the providence of Almighty God, will contribute something toward arresting the multitudinous evils of drunkenness that in this age are sweeping over the land. [Applause.]

The great work upon which this Society has entered is a personal reform—a social warfare. Its battles will be bloodless, its victories will be tearless; but the contest is a fearful one, for it is a struggle with the vitiated appetites of our fallen nature—appetites that have left scars deeply furrowed on the face of humanity. In all the ages, among all the nations, drunkenness has conquered the mightiest intellects, the bravest hearts, and the noblest natures. Soldiers who have led their conquering legions over fields of victory, statesmen who have swayed the destinies of nations, philosophers who have stamped the impress of their genius upon the ages, orators who have held listening Senates in rapt admiration, scholars who have led under contribution the vast domains of matter and of mind, have been the victims of intemperance. [Applause.]

It is estimated that in our own country, in this age of light and of knowledge, in this land with fifty thousand churches and fifty thousand ministers of the living God, we have an army of five hundred thousand drunkards; that fifty thousand of this army annually sink into drunkards' graves; that its ranks are kept filled by drafts upon the vast reserves of moderate drinkers. An army of half a million drunkards in Christian America! Every annual circuit of the sun fifty thousand new-made drunkards' graves! The perishing ranks of drunkenness recruited and crowded by merciless drafts upon the manhood of the nation! 'How fearful is the thought! How appalling the spectacle! Look at that army as it staggers on to annihilation. You see no mighty columns of heroes marching on with radiant banners, glad music, and glittering steel, to victory and to glory; but a multitudinous throng, broken, disordered, spiritless, tramping on to their doom, with the cries of fathers, mothers, brothers, sisters, wives, children, ringing in their ears. All ages and conditions are there—youth prematurely blighted; manhood broken, hopeless; age bending beneath the burdens of nameless sorrows; the generous, the noble, men of heart, of mind. and of soul, struggling in the grasp of drunkenness like giants in chains; but their feet ever glide onward and downward. God pity that throng of scarred, perishing, vanishing humanity. [Applause.]

It is our purpose, ladies and gentlemen, to hold ourselves back from this great army of drunkards—from this vast throng of moderate drinkers, upon whom drunkenness makes its annual drafts. It is our purpose, too, with the smile of God, to rescue the perishing drunkard and save the moderate drinker. We indulge the hope that this Congressional Society, by the blessing of Almighty God, will contribute something to this holy purpose, to rescue the fallen and save the falling. Let us, gentlemen of this Society, which we trust will long continue to enroll among its members the representatives of the people as they shall come hither in the years to come, be true to our plighted faith to each other, and to our vows to our God. [Applause.] Let us ever remember that strength comes from striving; that, in striving to rescue our fallen brothers, and to save our falling brothers from impending ruin, we may keep our own steps from gliding downward. Ever watching, and ever striving, when life's labors are done, our bodies may return to our mother earth unscarred, and our spirits to God who gave them, unstained by drunkenness. [Applause.]

LADIES AND GENTLEMEN—I have now the honor to present to you the Hon. HIRAM PRICE, of Iowa, an honored member of the House, and the President of the State Temperance Society of the young commonwealth of Iowa.

ADDRESS OF HON. HIRAM PRICE,

Of Iowa.

LADIES AND GENTLEMEN—For twenty-five years of my life, by word and act, at home and abroad, through evil and good report, by legal and by moral suasion, in season and (if such a thing be possible) out of season, I have, to the utmost of my ability and extent of my influence, endeavored to stand up for the cause of total abstinence, and the overthrow of intemperance. In the progress of this cause in the years of the past, the prospect of success has most generally been obscured by dark clouds of danger and defeat. Occasionally, however, the sunlight of success has, through rifts in those clouds, flecked the pathway, and cheered the hearts of the laborers in this cause. Never, in my most sanguine moments, did I anticipate such a scene as this hour presents. Here at the Capitol, in the high council chamber of the nation, the Senators and Representatives of a powerful and enlightened people have assembled for the purpose of devising ways and means for the overthrow of the enemy of our race, and for the upbuilding of the most glorious cause, save one, that ever engaged the hearts and hands of the children of men. [Applause.]

In the brief space of ten minutes, which, according to arrangement, is all that is allowed me, I can not, of course, attempt an argument, nor is argument necessary. An attempt to prove that intemperance is a master vice, would be a work of supererogation. That fact is proven by the thousands of wives who are worse than widows, and the tens of thousands of children who are worse than orphans; nor is there a man or woman within the sound of my voice who is not willing to admit that intemperance is an evil destructive of soul and body.

The question to be considered, then, is, what shall be done to stay this tide of evil, wretchedness, and misery? There are but two classes of persons on this question—those who practice total abstinence, and those who do not; or I might class them again, as total abstinence men, moderate drinkers, and those who have got a step beyond, and are now standing on the verge of a drunkard's grave. But for the present I shall only range them in the first two classes. Of that vast army of five hundred thousand drunkards, which it is said our land now contains, and of which number the State of Pennsylvania alone furnishes, according to a recent statement, between thirty and forty thousand, not one came from the ranks of the total abstinence men, but all, every one, from the ranks of the moderate drinkers. If all men and women were reliable, thorough-going, uncompromising total abstinence men and women, no more recruits could be obtained for this army of drunkards, and this curse would be removed. Therefore the object of all temperance societies, strictly so-called, is to take from the enemy that source of strength, and

make all men total abstinence men, for outside of that there
is no safety.

No total abstinence man or woman becomes a drunkard,
but the drunkards do all come from the ranks of the moderate drinkers, and therefore any man who is a moderate
drinker is responsible, to a certain extent, for the increase
of drunkenness and drunkards in the land. If time would
allow, I should like to dwell longer upon that point, for there
is the danger, and there is where the enemy finds his strength,
his life, and power for evil.

If you stand by the bedside of the poor drunkard who has
lost all for time and eternity, he will tell you, if he tells the
truth (and he will be very likely to do so under these circumstances), that he commenced by drinking some of the lighter
beverages, such as cider, beer, ale, porter, etc., and that step
by step he advanced in the downward path to ruin, until he
has reached his present position. Hence the necessity for
total abstinence organizations to counteract the drinking
usages of society, and shed the sunlight of happiness on the
dark places of the earth.

All other plans have failed; half-way measures will not
reach the case, but practical, consistent, total abstinence
never can fail. I appeal to you, then, as sensible, candid,
thinking men, to say whether it is not always safer to engage
in a measure that can not possibly fail, rather than take any
risk where the hazard is so tremendous.

My fellow-citizens, I want to say to you, and particularly
to the Senators and Representatives assembled here to-night,
that a responsibility rests upon you, because of this occasion,
that never rested upon you before. The first Napoleon proclaimed to his men, that forty centuries looked down upon
them from the Pyramids. I say to you, that this night, more
than thirty millions of free people, whose representatives you

are, are looking to your action, and anxious to know whether you will stand firm or not. At the first bugle blast for the call of this Congressional Temperance Society, forty-five men enrolled their names and rallied around the temperance flag, and the number each day is increasing. We have hung our banner on the outer wall, and proclaimed to the world that while we live we will drink no more intoxicating liquors. [Applause.]

I appeal to you as legislators, as fellow-citizens, as men engaged in the same great cause; I appeal to you by all that you call sacred in the present, and all that you expect in the future, to stand firm in this cause, so that those who behold your actions may be constrained to believe that there is stability in the Congressional Temperance Society, formed at the Capitol of our Nation, at the high noon of the nineteenth century. I adjure you by the recollections of the past, by all the scenes of wretchedness and misery that lie along the pathway of each of your past histories, to stand firm. Remember your pledge; remember that if you touch but a drop to your lips, a vast ocean may surround you, an ocean fathomless and shoreless, from which there is no escape.

In this cause there is ample room for the exercise of the noblest faculties and the brightest genius, in persuading men and women to abandon the wine cup and drink only that beverage which was prepared by God Himself to nourish and invigorate His creatures and to beautify His footstool; that which gives life and beauty and usefulness to the golden harvests, the magnificent forests, and whatever else on earth that blooms or beautifies, and without which all must wither, droop, and die.

· And now, the few moments allowed me for these remarks having expired, my last words are, sign the total abstinence pledge, and keep it while time endures. [Applause.]

1*

ADDRESS OF HON. SAMUEL McKEE,

Of Kentucky.

LADIES AND GENTLEMEN—I have not the experience of the gentleman who has preceded me in this meeting. I have not for twenty-five years been a temperance lecturer. I have not, furthermore, until the present session of Congress, ever belonged to a temperance society; but I am not, as you might infer if I stopped here, a very recent convert to the cause of temperance, for since my boyhood, since the day I left my father's house to go out into the world to battle for myself, I have put away from me altogether all kinds of intoxicating liquors. I believed then, as I know now by experience, what my friend has said so well, that this is the only safe course for a man to pursue in order to pass on to honor and attain that high position which the Creator intended for man when He launched him into the world. And my short experience in public life, and mingling in the world, has taught me, if I had not believed it before, that this thing of intemperance is the ruin and destruction, the utter loss of more gallant and noble men than all other evils in the world combined. That being the case, it certainly ought to be the highest aim of all men—aye, of all women, too, for in this work, as well as all others, the influence of woman is all-powerful, and generally, perhaps always intentionally, the influence of woman is on the side of good—to give encouragement to this work. Woman oftentimes, like other mortals, commits blunders, and I believe that a great deal of the drunkenness that exists in this land grows out of the encouragement of those men who are generally recognized in society as "good fellows"—lively, jolly young men, who generally seem to be preferred, from some cause or other, by the ladies, to quiet, sober men. Now this is not as it should be. If you find a good, lively, social kind of man, of course encourage him; but when you find that man wandering away to those places where men are so apt to go in order to stimulate themselves for lively work, let your voice follow that man, and let it ring in his ears, " *Come back, come back ; death is in that door !*"

Of course at a meeting of this kind, and where so many men are called upon to address you, it is not expected we shall say much. Much may be done by example, and I am glad to hear the warning from my friend, to stand by what we have undertaken; and I may be pardoned for making one remark right here, and say that, so far as his remark applied to the present Congress, the conduct of this Congress has already taught the nation that it goes not backward on any advance it has made. [Applause.]

I know it is the custom among all men throughout all lands to use these rumsellers, these whisky shops, these men who deal in this article, as promoters of their prospects when they stand before the people. Nothing is more pernicious, more wrong, or so unnecessary. I have heard, in my short experience, of men giving a very large bonus to certain keepers of coffee-houses, that they may throw their influence for them in election times. In my own State it has been the custom to use this as one of the chief means of promoting the chances of a candidate and winning the people—more so, perhaps, than in the New England or Middle States. But such a course in my own State I believe to be entirely unnecessary. It adds nothing to their chances of success, and men generally are apt to close the canvass and find the expense they have gone to has been thrown away, because the men are not to be trusted who deal in it. I relate you simply my own experi-

ence in this matter—not because it is mine, but simply as an
example—when I was a candidate before my people—and it
was the only time I have ever been a candidate for a political
office in my life—although it had been the custom there,
whenever a candidate came, to set out a free drinking establishment. When I began the canvass in my own district, at
almost the first place I visited I was approached by one of
these men for money, that he could "treat" all his friends.
"That is the way," he said, "to get votes." "Well," said I
to my friends, "if that be the way to secure votes, I shall
never secure any. I drink no liquor." [Applause.] I made
the canvass through my district on that theory. On the last
day but one before the election, dining with an old gentleman,
an acquaintance of mine, who had long been a politician in
the State of Kentucky, said he, "What are your prospects
for election?" I said, "I feel that I shall be elected." "How
have you conducted this campaign?" Said I, "On strict
principles of honesty, treating nobody, spending no money
anywhere except it was necessary to send a man to the polls
who could not get there without means." He looked strangely
at me, and with a rather saddened countenance said, "You
will not be elected. I have been a politician in Kentucky too
long, and I never knew a man conduct a canvass on that scale
to succeed." But he was deceived. The election proved the
contrary. And if I have been the first candidate to conduct
a campaign successfully on that theory, in all other canvasses,
I pledge you and the people, they shall be conducted in the
same way. [Applause.] I know not whether there be a
band of five hundred thousand marching to drunkards' graves
or not; I dare say the Chairman has not over-estimated the
amount. But to-day I have learned, from an organization
which has done an immense amount of good, that in the city
of New York there are fifty thousand wandering, homeless,

houseless little ones; and I also state the fact, in connection with that, that three fourths of this number are made so by this course of intemperance, and by this sale of the vilest compound of liquor. Stringent laws may be enacted which will somewhat curb the evil; but the one great thing we need more than all that, is to educate the minds of the people— bring them up to that high sense of duty and honor that they will neither encourage nor countenance the men who make this a traffic; and when we have educated the minds of the people up to that point, we shall have no difficulty whatever in treating the matter. [Applause.]

ADDRESS OF HON. RICHARD YATES,

Of Illinois.

LADIES AND GENTLEMEN—It was not my intention to address you at all until this afternoon, and I feel the need of more preparation before speaking to so large an audience as this. The reason why I did not propose to address this assembly was because having so recently associated myself with the Congressional Temperance Association, I did not like to make a parade of myself before the public. Men sometimes sign pledges, and they break them; but, Mr. President, I have signed for good [applause], and I have made my covenant with God that I will keep mine. But I felt it were better to prove first that I was well established in my new position, before I attempted to express sentiments on this question in that earnest and enthusiastic manner in which I always address my fellow-citizens in behalf of any cause which has the conviction of my judgment and the approval of my heart.

Some two months ago your distinguished chairman, the able and eloquent Senator from Massachusetts, in his kindness, in the goodness of his great big heart, came to me with a petition numerously signed by members of Congress, and said: "Governor, I want you to sign a call for a temperance meeting." "With all my heart," said I. I signed it. But the temperance meeting did not come off. I became impatient. I went to the honorable Senator and told him I was tired of waiting; could he not furnish me a pledge? He said he could to-morrow. The next day he furnished me with a printed pledge of the Congressional Temperance Society. I put it in my pocket, took it home, took it to my room, read it carefully, and, after one look to God and one to home, I signed the pledge. I raised myself to my full height, and I was FREE. [Great applause.] If I refer to myself in the remarks I have made, and which I intend to make, I assure you it is not from egotism, for I take no peculiar pride myself in having been addicted to the use of ardent spirits. But there is another reason why I feel permitted to refer to myself, and that is, because while I have considered that I was only a moderate drinker, it has been published all over the land that I was a drunkard.

Fellow-citizens, there was some truth in this, and there was a vast deal of error in it, too. I was addicted to drinking occasionally as a stimulus, as I supposed, to strengthen my nerves [laughter], and as a heightener of social joys. But, Mr. Chairman, differently from other men, I had a most unfortunate difficulty with myself, and that was, I had a wonderful facility, whenever I drank, of letting everybody know it. [Laughter.] My sprees were not frequent, but they were long and they were loud. [Laughter.] The grand prairies of Illinois did not furnish area enough for one of my forward movements. [Laughter.] That was not only the case; but whatever I have done for the last seventeen years—whether I had to make a speech to a political meeting; whether I spoke against the Nebraska bill upon the floor of this House; whether, as Governor, I wrote a message, or published a proclamation, or prorogued a secession Legislature [great applause], the universal charge of the opposite party was, that all these acts were done under the influence of whisky. [Laughter.] Now, fellow-citizens, I have concluded to put a stop to this matter. The editors and reporters of newspapers are an honorable class of gentlemen whom I respect; but I want those libelous scribblers who have made so many misrepresentations as to my course of conduct, to understand that from this time henceforward their vocation in that respect is gone [laughter and applause], and they may now publish their libels until the hand that writes them shall fall withered and palsied; but I never intend that they shall have any license or authority to publish me as a drunkard again, even if I have to abstain, as I will abstain, from the mildest glass of claret that ever the fair hand of the fairest lady in this land should present to me. [Applause.]

There is the evil of the thing—this misrepresentation, this liability to misrepresentation. Why, sir, after I had made these speeches, some sharp article of abuse would be published in the paper, and some " Friendly Indian" of mine [laughter] would mark around it with black lines and send it to me for my Christian contemplation and supreme delight. [Laughter.] I will stop it. I have promised God; I have promised my country; I have promised that proud Commonwealth which for twenty-five consecutive years has honored me with all her public positions, in the Legislature, as Governor, as member of both Houses of Congress; I have promised all who love me, and I have promised Katie and the children [loud applause], that I will never touch, taste, nor handle the unclean thing [applause]; and by the blessing of God and my own unfaltering purpose, I intend to fight it out on this line to the last day in the evening of my life. [Applause.] If all you, gentlemen, would do the same thing, you would lose nothing in mind, body, or estate. [Laughter.]

Fellow-citizens: It may seem strange, but I would, as I feel now, as soon drink fire from hell as whisky, for it is hell and damnation, too. It destroys the health, and mars the beauty of the body; it can bow down to earth the most giant intellect, and make it weak as that of a child. It demoralizes and it annihilates the immortal soul. It makes a man forget his children or the wife of his bosom, and treat them with harsh unkindness and barbarity, and even murder them. Unaffected by intemperance, he would peril his life for that wife of his love; he would dive into the ocean's depths, face the cannon's mouth, or peril his life amid the flames of the burning dwelling to snatch from death his darling babe.

I do not suppose at all that I am superior to anybody else in intellect. I certainly have no special claims to consideration from birth or fortune. But there is one thing I do claim, and that is, that God has endowed me with nobility of soul, with warm and generous impulses—a heart as unfathomable in its affections as the ocean, and as broad as the area of humanity; and I appeal to you, Mr. Chairman, from our slight acquaintance, if you do not think I have enough of the *ardent* about me without *ardent spirits*. [Laughter.]

Mr. WILSON.—Yes; you have.

Mr. YATES.—I would say to the young man, that grandeur of human character does not consist of transcendant genius alone. It does not belong alone to the statesman beneath whose eloquence listening Senates sit enraptured; it does not belong alone to the warrior who bears his proud, unconquered banner over every field ; but it does consist in force of character, in force of soul, feeling, thought, and purpose. Cæsar was a weak man when he sacrificed the liberties of Rome by suffering Mark Antony to put the crown upon his head. Washington would not have been great if he had yielded to the temptations of his willing army and accepted a crown at the expense of the liberties of his country. The reformed drunkard accomplishes a more heroic achievement than did the Spartan band at Thermopylæ, because he conquers himself. That man is only great who seeks right and truth and justice, and adheres to them with strong, vigorous, and perpetual purpose.

As to the effects upon the nation, Mr. Jefferson said, many years ago :

" The habit of using alcoholic liquors by men in office has created more injury to the public service, and given more trouble to me than any other circumstance which has occurred in the internal concerns of the country during my administration. If I had to commence my administration again, with the knowledge I have from experience derived, the first question which I would ask from a candidate for public favor would be, is he addicted to the use of ardent spirits ?"

The man who is to legislate for a great country, to help make laws and constitutions involving the destinies of millions of human beings, ought to be a man of reflection, moral principle, integrity, and, above all, a sober man. [Applause.] Go into your legislative halls, State and national, and behold the drunkard staggering to his seat or sleeping at his post, and ask yourself the question, whether he is not more fit to be called a monument of his country's shame than the representative of freemen ? Would it not be most fearful to contemplate that ill-fated epoch in the history of our country

when the demon of intemperance shall come into our legislative halls without shame, remorse, or rebuke; when he shall
sit upon juries, upon the bench, and drunkenness run riot
among the people. Who then will protect the ship of state
upon this maddening tide; who will steer her in her onward
course amid the dashing billows; who spread her starry flag
to the free, fresh, wild winds of heaven?

Watchman, what of the night? We have been engaged
in a mighty revolution. Your army and navy have carried
your arms under Grant and Banks against the Gibraltars of
the Mississippi, and opened that stream from its source to its
mouth. Under the gallant Joe Hooker your troops scaled
the heights, and above the clouds unfurled to the sun the
glorious flag of the stars. [Applause.] Sherman marches
from Cairo to the sea, while Grant marches through the
Wilderness to the Confederate capital. The rebellion is
crushed. Behold! a whole race set free—the shackles of the
ages are broken, and we see full-high advanced the standard
of the nation's redemption. "Hark! dinna ye hear the
pibroch of the Highlanders?" and borne upon the wings of
the wind the slogan shout of universal emancipation?
[Applause.]

And now shall this puissant nation, "Columbia, queen of
the world and child of the skies," pause in her efforts when
there is an enemy in our land more destructive than war,
pestilence, and famine combined, which sends annually one
hundred thousand men to untimely graves, makes fifty
thousand widows, and three hundred thousand wives worse
than widows—filling our prisons, our poor-houses, our lunatic
asylums, and swelling to an untold extent the great ocean of
human misery, wretchedness, and woe?

Somebody told me he saw in a Chicago paper the other
day, that since Governor Yates had joined the temperance

society, whisky had fallen ten cents a gallon. [Laughter.]
Well, that's good, indeed. [Laughter.] At all events, it's
good news, for all that ever kept my slanderers from drinking
themselves to death *pro bono publico*, was the high price of
whisky. [Laughter.] We will bring it within their reach,
for it will have to fall much lower than the present price
before it reaches its real intrinsic value—a specie basis.
[Laughter.] Mr. President, if old King Alcohol were dead
and buried, as he ought to be, beyond the power of resurrec-
tion, this nation could bear our national debt like a young
Hercules. [Applause.] Then, sir, two blades of grass would
grow where one now grows, and unbounded wealth, imperial
power, and proud position would be the heritage of the nation
forever. [Applause.]

But some say this temperance business is fanaticism—it's a
gloomy sort of life. There never was a greater mistake.
Temperance is one of the sweetest and most delightful things
upon earth; it is the very spring-head of cheerfulness, happiness, and joy—the very chivalry of manhood itself. I have
been a temperance man for fifteen days, and I am a gayer
boy to-night than I have been for seventeen years. [Laugh-
ter.] I think I am the gayest man in the Senate, except the
compeer of Clay and Crittenden—the able, indomitable, and
gallant old cavalier of Kentucky (Garrett Davis). I except
you also, Mr. Chairman. [Laughter.] Temperance gloomy?
Not a bit of it, Mr. President. My pledge shall be a perpetual charm—"a thing of beauty which is a joy forever"—
not a cloud of gloom, but an ever-present rainbow of promise,
hope, and beauty. I am as proud of it as of my wife and
children, and that is the strongest way I have to express my
pride. [Applause.] I am as proud of it as I am of the commission which entitles me to hold the position of an American
Senator. By-the-by, Mr. Chairman, I will submit to you the

question: I rather think the commission and the temperance pledge ought to go together. [Applause.] What do you think about having "the teetotaler" put into the iron-clad oath? [Laughter.]

You say, of what use is the pledge? I will tell you. Twenty days ago there came along a friend of mine—a Senator—and said, "Let us take a drink." I said, "Certainly—all right." Another friend from Illinois in about three minutes and a half came along and said, "Let us take a drink." Said I, "All right." It is this way: One drink of liquor is enough for me; two ain't half enough [laughter]; three is only one third enough, and four is chaos. After I signed the pledge I was asked several times to drink, but I didn't do any such thing. [Laughter.]

After I signed this temperance pledge, I wrote to a little lady out in Illinois, who weighs about a hundred pounds, has black hair and flashing black eyes, and "a form fairer than Grecian chisel ever woke from Parian marble," and I received the following answer: "MY DEAR RICHARD—How beautiful is this morning! how bright the sun shines! how sweetly our birds sing! how joyous the children! how happy is my heart! I see the smile of God. He has answered the prayer. Always proud of your success, you have now achieved that success which God and angels will bless. It is the shining summit of human aspiration, for you have conquered yourself. All who love you will aid you to keep the pledge. I love you, my dear boy!   KATIE."

"Love, the sun, soul, and center of the moral universe;
  Love, which links angel to angel and God to man;
  Love, which binds in one two loving hearts. *How beautiful is love!*"

As I look over this audience, composed of Senators and Representatives of this great nation, and these galleries blazing with beauty and the worth of the city, and sojourners from all the States and Territories, I ask myself why they are here. Proud England, upon whose dominions the sun never sets, has but one queen, but, thank God, we have millions of queens, who

> " Shine in beauty like the night
> Of sunny climes and starry skies !"

whose chains we feel, and yet we bless the silken scepter. . You are here to give by your presence encouragement to the Congressional Temperance Society, and I propose, sir, that this Society shall be the beginning of societies throughout the land, and that we will push forward the temperance column, move upon the enemy's works, and give him canister and Greek fire. [Applause.] We will storm upon the citadel of intemperance until it shall crumble and totter and fall to the earth. [Applause.] Why do I refer to the ladies? Because their example is mightier than the eloquence of a thousand Senates or the banners of a thousand legions.

You are here to-night to see the snowy white flag of temperance as it is unfurled over the Capitol of your country, as it rises and rises, and unfolds to God and spreads until it shall cover the whole land, and until there shall not be a drunkard nor a moderate drinker to take away the bloom from the cheek of female beauty, and until all the hearthstones of this land shall blaze with comfort and joy, and happiness and gladness shall dwell in green freshness there. [Tremendous applause.]

ADDRESS OF HON. F. E. WOODBRIDGE,

Of Vermont.

IT is, of course, quite impossible, in the few moments which it will be proper for me to occupy, to enter upon any discussion in treating the great moral and social question which has brought so many of us together this evening. Indeed, I suppose the meeting was not called for the purpose of going over old and worn-out arguments in favor of abstinence from intoxicating drinks, but rather to stir one another up by way of remembrance, and enkindle a new enthusiasm, and awaken a new zeal.

Now, I have no experience to narrate—certainly I am not one of the old apostles who have grown gray in the service. I joined the Congressional Temperance Society because I thought it would be best for myself, my children, and for those who may look to me for an example, or over whom I may exert the least influence. And again, the time is propitious for the advancement of every moral and social enterprise. For the last few years we have thought of nothing but the terrible war which has devastated our beloved country, deluged the land with blood, and brought lamentation and mourning to all our households. Sweet peace has dawned—the passions of men are more or less subdued; purer purposes and influences are working upon the individual and upon society, and the heart seems to long for something better and holier than bloody and cruel war. Hence it would seem, from the condition of things, that it is the day for progress, and, in my judgment, the earnest, thoughtful laborer for the good of his fellow-man will reap an abundant harvest, which, in the last great day, will add new jewels to his crown of rejoicing.

Man is a splendid creature! God thought so when He created him. God thought so when He gave His only and well-beloved Son—our blessed Saviour—to die for him. The earth, with its magnificence of beauty,—the heavens, with their indescribable glories, were made for man; and when God breathed into the nostrils of His image His own breath of life, everything was so perfect and glorious that the morning stars sang together for joy.

The sun, as it walks in majesty through the heavens, gives light, and heat, and life; the little violet at our feet, which tells us that spring-time and the singing of birds is coming; the stars, as they dazzle and sparkle in the sky; and the little fire-fly, as it lights up the swamps at night, were all made for the benefit and comfort of man. How great, then, is the' dignity of manhood! and how fearful are its responsibilities! Whatever thought, whatever act, whatever purpose, what- ever habit detracts from that dignity is wrong. Whatever course of action fails to meet those high responsibilities is also wrong. Hence the propriety, and even the necessity, of temperance, and hence, also, the duty of action, vigorous, kindly, loving effort to raise up those who have yielded to temptation, and to prevent the young man from falling into the fatal snare.

Young man, you feel that you are safe. Perhaps you have never been intoxicated. You only take a social glass with your genial friends—all of them gentlemanly and upright young men—after the labors of the day are over. Many a young man, with a mind as well poised, with as much self-control, with as gentlemanly habits and purpose of thought and action as you now have, have been in the same position. Where are they now? Gone to an untimely and dishonored grave, leaving behind them blasted hopes, sad memories, and broken hearts.

Men are creatures of habit. "Excess of appetite doth grow by what it feeds on." You know, and I know, that, as a general rule, the habit creeps upon one with an insidious, noiseless tread. He that takes a glass to-day, must take two to-morrow, and then three, and four, and five, and six, and, ere he knows it, the serpent's coil is about him, and he becomes the almost hopeless and despairing victim of intemperance. See how it is with other habits. Take the use of tobacco. When I first used it, it was disgusting; it made me sick; but, thinking it to be manly, I persevered, amid vomitings and cramps, until I could smoke without nausea. I thought I was a man. Now what is the result? To-day I am a slave to the abominable habit, and would give a good Vermont farm to be rid of it. It may be difficult to account for this, but the fact exists.

Then, why put yourself in this danger? You do not require the stimulant now; you are in the midst of your manly pride and strength. Then taste not, touch not, handle not, lest by-and-by it biteth like a serpent and stingeth like an adder!

I would like to talk to the ladies a little as to their duty—for it is always pleasant for a gentleman to talk to the purest and most beautiful part of creation—but time will not permit.

It is sometimes said that it is almost useless to endeavor to reform the confirmed inebriate, and that our efforts must be devoted to the prevention rather than the cure. I do not think so. Men's hearts seem to be hardened against the unfortunate victim of this inexorable habit. They are apt to say, "Oh, he is a miserable drunkard; let him go!" Sir, that man may once have been as good as you or I; and, saving that unfortunate habit, he may, in the eye of God,

who sees not as men see, be as good or better than you or I
to-day. When himself, he may be good to the poor, kind
and loving to his family, obedient to the law, respectful to the
ordinances of religion. I confess, sir, when I see a drunken
man, my impulse is to go to him and kindly lead him to a
place of safety. Think a moment! He is our brother; God
made him; Christ died for him, and knocks at his heart, as
He does at ours, for admission. Think again of the wife,
who, in the freshness and beauty of her early youth, pledged
this man her love, and, with that fidelity which kept woman
last at the cross and brought her first at the tomb, clings to him
now. Think of her prayers, ascending like pure incense to her
heavenly Father, that her husband may be reclaimed. Think,
too, of those little children watching at the window, when
night has fallen, for the approaching shadow of their father,
or listening for his footsteps, refusing to leave their dear
mother until he is in safety. Think, too, of the prayers and
groans of this unfortunate man, as in the darkness and still-
ness of midnight he pleads to be delivered from this terrible
woe.; and as in the morning he leaves his home, his children
cover him with kisses, and the face of his wife lights up as
with an angel's smile, as he promises to drink no more. He
is honest in that promise, but the tempter comes and he falls
again. Revile not, upbraid not that poor unfortunate man!
Rather lift him up with kindness and encouragement from
the pit into which he has fallen. Show him the dignity of
his own nature, the beauty of truth, and purity, and sobriety,
and bid him go and sin no more. If he falls again, and perhaps he may, once more put your arms around him, and by-
and-by he may become clothed and in his right mind, and be
once again a man. If there is joy in heaven over one sinner
that repenteth, is it not worth while for man to save one soul
from a drunkard's grave? The happiness of life is reflex. It

2

comes from without, and not from within. To do good is to be happy.

Let us, then, in this and in all things, strive to promote the welfare of our brother man, and then, when kind hands smooth for the last time our pillow, as we are about to close our eyes forever upon earth, we may say, "When the eye saw me thus, it blessed me. When the ear heard me, it gave witness to me—for I delivered the poor that cried; the fatherless and him that had none to help him; the blessing of him that was ready to perish came upon me, and I caused the widow's heart to sing for joy." [Applause.]

ADDRESS OF HON. WM. E. DODGE,

Of New York.

As I have sat, sir, looking at this interesting spectacle, I have asked myself, why are we assembled here to-night?. Is it in view of the approach of some epidemic? Is the cholera just upon us, and have we met here to-night to consult as to what measures may be taken to stay the progress of the dire plague? No, sir; we are met here to-night in view of a wide-spread evil more to be dreaded than the cholera. More die in a single year from the influence of intoxicating drinks than all who have perished from cholera since the year 1832, when it first visited our land. If we had met here to consult as to staying the progress of the cholera, what would be said to one who should stand up and declare that he had a panacea that he could present as a remedy to stay the progress of this scourge? But we are here, sir, in view of this terrible evil, to present to this audience a panacea as sure and certain as that the individual who shall take it, abide by its instructions and follow the directions given for its use.

We are here to contemplate the fact already stated, that there are fifty thousand persons going annually to drunkards' graves. Mr. President, I fully indorse this—not that all die admitted drunkards, but they die premature deaths from disease superinduced by the use of intoxicating drinks. The friends and the physician know what was the cause, but report says "heart disease," "dropsy," or "apoplexy," while tens of thousands die absolute drunkards. We talk of fifty thousand! The last few years have taught us numericals as we have never understood them before. Fifty thousand! Can we comprehend it? Never, until these years of war, has there been an army of fifty thousand collected in our land. Some of us stood on this beautiful avenue two years ago, and for long hours witnessed the long columns of our returning noble veterans as they passed in review. But, as we stood there, could we have realized, as we looked upon their faces, that they were all marching to drunkards' graves, with what terrible anxiety should we have viewed them! But, sir, if when that mighty army of fifty thousand had passed down to drunkards' graves, we could feel that that was the end of the procession, it would not be so terrible. But as 1868 looms up in the distance, we behold the onward march of fifty thousand more coming from those licensed places for recruit. ing drunkards—the hotels and saloons. I wish I could stop here; but they come not only from the saloons, hotels, and drinking-shops, but they come enlisted from the dining-tables of the distinguished men of our land, where temptation is set before them because it is fashionable, and where they drink because it is unfashionable not to drink; they come from where parties assemble, where the punch-bowl is seen, where intoxicating drinks circulate amid our wives, our mothers, sisters, and friends, and where temptation meets the man who enters that house with the determination not to drink; where the young and lovely female reaches out the tempting glass, and there is not moral courage to resist, and so he enlists and makes one of that mighty coming throng. I say nothing here of the habit as it fastens itself, in such circumstances, on many a lovely woman. Facts could be given which would startle those who set temptation in the way of the unsuspecting.

I said, sir, we had a panacea. It is nothing more nor less than the very thing the noble Senator has done, which is, to sign the pledge and stop drinking. [Applause.] What is that pledge? Allow me to read it, and if I had time I should like to read the names of the noble men who have signed it.

"We, the undersigned, members of the Senate and House of Representatives of the United States, do agree that we will not use intoxicating liquors as a beverage, nor traffic in them; that we will not provide them as an article of entertainment, or for persons in our employment; and that in all suitable ways we will discountenance their use throughout the community."

After the reading of the pledge, which was received with applause, the names of the signers were called for by the audience, and were read by Mr. Dodge, as follows:

SENATORS.

Henry Wilson, of Mass.	E. G. Ross, of Kansas.
Richard Yates, of Illinois.	L. M. Morrill, of Maine.
W. T. Willey, of W. Virginia.	A. H. Cragin, of N. Hampshire.
S. C. Pomeroy, of Kansas.	W. Saulsbury, of Delaware.

REPRESENTATIVES.

Schuyler Colfax, of Indiana.	G. W. Julian, of Indiana.
H. Price, of Iowa.	S. M. Cullom, of Illinois.
T. A. Plants, of Ohio.	A. A. Barker, of Pennsylvania.
S. Perham, of Maine.	R. E. Trowbridge, of Michigan.

REPRESENTATIVES.

J. B. Grinnell, of Iowa.
W. B. Washburn, of Mass.
T. W. Ferry, of Michigan.
W. Windom, of Minnesota.
B. C. Cook, of Illinois.
C. Delano, of Ohio.
J. W. Patterson, of N. H.
J. T. Holmes, of New York.
John Wentworth, of Illinois.
S. F. Wilson, of Pennsylvania.
W. A. Newell, of New Jersey.
S. McKee, of Kentucky.
C. T. Hulburd, of New York.
John Lynch, of Maine.
John H. Rice, of Maine.
W. Lawrence, of Ohio.
J. H. D. Henderson, of Oregon.
H. L. Dawes, of Massachusetts.

A. Van Aernam, of New York.
J. H. Hubbard, of Connecticut.
J. B. Alley, of Massachusetts.
Amasa Cobb, of Wisconsin.
P. Sawyer, of Wisconsin.
F. E. Woodbridge, of Vermont.
Charles Upson, of Michigan.
W. Higby, of California.
J. W. McClurg, of Missouri.
O. Ames, of Massachusetts.
W. E. Dodge, of New York.
L. W. Ross, of Illinois.
W. D. McIndoe, of Wisconsin.
H. S. Bundy, of Ohio.
J. F. Benjamin, of Missouri.
C. D. Hubbard, of W. Virginia.
J. R. Kelso, of Missouri.

Mr. Dodge.—Mr. President, I should like to know if that is to come out of my time? [Laughter.]

Mr. Wilson.—You have left out one name that ought not to be left out—that is the name of Thaddeus Stevens. [Great applause.]

Mr. Dodge.—I will say in regard to that name, that that gentleman said to me on Saturday evening, that if he was well enough to be out of bed he would certainly be here, if he did no more than to say that for thirty years he never had drank a drop of anything which could intoxicate. [Applause.]

Now, sir, I was speaking of the panacea. When we offer this panacea, we ought not to be called fanatics. We are not fanatics. We offer a simple, philosophic remedy for the most terrible calamity and disease. How simple! The patient has not the cholera, yellow fever, or consumption, but he has a habit of using stimulating drinks. We are not fanatics, although no man can take the Bible in his hand and say to me that *per se* it is sin for me to drink wine. Yet he *can* take that Bible and show most conclusively that there may be circumstances under which it would be sin for me to drink. If my brother had been addicted to the use of intoxi- cating drinks, and was manfully struggling to resist the appetite (which none but they who have acquired it know), should I drink my wine in his presence, put it on my table and ask him to drink, and he should be overcome, and die a drunkard, God would call me to account for my brother's blood. And who is my brother? God tells us who. Our neighbors — all over whom we have influence — are our brothers; and when we set on our table the deadly cup, and put it to our neighbors' lips, we are doing that which, per- chance, will lead some struggling brother to go down to a drunkard's grave, to meet us at the judgment and charge us with his ruin. And now, Mr. President, comes in the power of sympathy and example, which is the grand foundation of every temperance organization. It is simply the Bible prin- ciple which we should endeavor to follow—self-sacrifice for the good of others. Paul said: "It is neither good to eat flesh, nor drink wine, nor anything which shall cause my brother to stumble or to fall. If meat make my brother to offend, I will eat no more meat while the world stands, lest I make my brother to offend." That is the doctrine. [Applause.]

Mr. Van Meter here brought in ten young girls from the New York Home for little wanderers, who sang, "Dear Father, Come Home!"

Mr. DODGE.—Ah! Mr. President, who can think of the broken hearts, and the desolate and ruined homes, and not sympathize with that wife or parent when those they love so tenderly "do come home," bringing the evidence that they have enlisted in this army? And now let me say, before sitting down, to my fellow-members of the Thirty-ninth Congress: the eye of the nation rests upon this Congress as the focal point. Whatever emanates from this Congress goes world-wide. We are here placed high upon the mount of responsibility, and as we have, by God's blessing, helped to save the nation from that terrible curse of slavery, is there a man here who will not be willing to sacrifice himself for the sake of saving the fifty thousand who are to die in 1868, and to save the nation? [Applause.]

ADDRESS OF HON. SCHUYLER COLFAX,

Of Indiana.

Mr. PRESIDENT, LADIES, AND GENTLEMEN—The President of this society solicited me a day or two ago to speak at this first meeting of the Congressional Temperance Society, and although I tried to decline, yet, when he pressed the argument upon me that every one should be ready to give a reason for the faith that is in him, duty seemed to require that I should speak to you, though it will be but briefly. Why should we not speak for such a cause—not banded together for honors, for office, for wealth or fame, but to plead affectionately in behalf of hundreds of thousands of worse than orphan children, like those you have just listened to, "Dear father, come home." My devotion to this cause, and my interest in it, dates back years further than the signing of any written pledge. My mind turns back to-night from this brilliant audience in this council hall of the nation to a scene

over twenty years ago, when I first stepped on the threshold
of manhood. I stood by the death-bed of a young friend—
of the same temperament, of the same habits, associations,
and surroundings as myself—in that Western State to which
I had emigrated, and there witnessed that saddest of all
scenes, his soul tearing itself away from the clay tenement
which encased it, amid the wild ravings and agonizing shrieks
of that most terrible and fearful of all diseases, *delirium
tremens.* Fighting imaginary reptiles and demons, imprecat-
ing the name of his Creator, his soul passed away. And
there, at his death-bed, I resolved, God being my helper,
never to follow in the road that both of us had trodden up to
that time, but on which he had advanced so much more
rapidly than myself. [Applause.] This demon, insatiate
in its demands, finds its victims everywhere—the gifted as
well as the illiterate—the powerful as well as the humble—
the honorable as well as the debased; and sometimes, as
though, like Death, loving a shining mark, you find his trail
in the forum of the jurist, in the national halls of legislation—
aye, even in the sacred desk. The young man just starting
out on the pathway of an active life, the middle-aged, with
his mind ripened and matured, and even the venerable man,
tottering into the grave, are among the victims of this
insatiable monster. It is well, therefore, that we should
organize against him. More destructive than a hostile army
ravaging your land, for that strikes but at the life of your
body, while this strikes at the life of your soul. Most
especially wise, too, to organize here; for, if anywhere in this
broad land, the assembled Senators and Representatives who
are here in these halls to legislate for all the best interests of
this continental domain, washed by the two great oceans of
the globe, with the millions now within our jurisdiction, and
the millions who are yet to come when we have passed

away—here should they have clear heads and sober minds. And, sir, I am proud to say that from that chair for days, weeks, months, and even years, looking into the faces of my fellow-members here, I say, before God and my fellow-men, that in the twelve years of public service in this Capitol, I have never seen less intoxication dishonoring this Hall than in this Congress which is now closing. [Applause.] But, sir, as this monster sweeps on in his horrid triumph, he gathers his trophies everywhere. Go out into the broad land with me, and look upon them. You will find them in the squalid hovels bereft of every comfort. You will find them in starving, destitute, dependent families. You will find them in that ever-moving, never-ceasing procession going to the unhappy drunkards' grave; in the poor-houses throughout our land; in the penitentiaries, where the victim, branded by the very society that allowed him to be lured to his fall, atones with shaven head and felon garb for the crime he committed under the influence of intoxication. You will find its trophies on the gallows, with the victims hanging between heaven and earth, as if not fit for either; and, sad as all the rest, in the darkened intellects of those who survive.

If I had but a single word to say to the young before I closed, I would remind them of that striking remark of Pythagoras, the Samian sage, who said that the paths of virtue and vice were like the letter Y; starting from the same point, they soon diverge to the right and the left. These two pathways are before you as you enter into this stern conflict with life. One is broad and plain; with God's sunlight shining on your footsteps; but the other is full of stumbling-blocks, rugged and craggy with the tangled wild-wood, with hidden pitfalls and overhanging precipices, and when you start upon that road, God only knows what is to be your end.

2*

One gentleman to-night spoke about our personal duty to our fellow-men. Is it not devolving upon us, binding upon our hearts and consciences, and dare we turn away and leave our fellow-man as we see him hurrying down this declivity to what we know must be the end? No, sir. The answer comes to us as the question itself comes, through the procession of centuries from the birth-place of mankind, "Am I my brother's keeper, helper, guide, and friend?" There is one beautiful remark in the Alcoran of Mahomet, when speaking of cases like this, that approaches the doctrines we believe— that has in it the essence of true Christianity and advanced civilization even for this nineteenth century. Said Mahomet, "When a man dies, the people, as they bury him out of their sight, will ask, "What property has he left behind him? (and they do it to this day;) but the angels, as they bend over his grave, will inquire, What good deeds hast thou sent before thee?" Here is the cause in which you can gather up these good deeds, which shall shine like stars in the firmament forever. If you can turn back but one erring brother, oh, the happiness when you can feel that your own efforts have restored the bloom of happiness and of joy to the pallid cheek of her who was worse than widowed!

Leonidas, as Senator Yates has said, stood in the pass with his Spartan band, and by heroic self-sacrifice turned back the foe, and his fame and his name will live, from the rivers to the ends of the earth, forever. But if you stand in the pathway between sobriety and intemperance, and turn back your deluded and self-destroying brother-man, your glory in the Hereafter shall be brighter even than that of Leonidas, for you have saved not only your brother, but perhaps his undying soul. [Applause.]

ADDRESS OF HON. J. B. GRINNELL,

Of Iowa.

LADIES AND GENTLEMEN—In listening to the glowing pictures of restored men and society reformed, I am reminded of that incident in the classic era of Greece when it was proposed that there should be a monument erected and the lovers of art were invited to make a contribution to national glory, when Phidias. came forward to say, " What my brothers have proposed I have accomplished." Now I make no personal allusion, not being worthy of the compliment bestowed on me by the Chairman; yet I desire to say that I come from the State of Iowa, representing it in part in this House, and can say that in this cause I transfer all to her that has taken the lead in our cause of the States in this Union. I know you will rejoice to learn this of that young State, lying between the father and the mother of waters, beautiful in nature, grand in proportion, prosperous and growing, to be the fair abode for millions. A few years ago I left the city of New York, where I could not cross Broadway very conveniently, and went where I could, and where I need not be troubled with the chronic intemperance of that city. I found such a place on the prairies of Iowa. I made my home three miles from any inhabitant. Taking possession of a little tract of land there, we laid out a town, and said to ourselves, by the blessing of God there shall never be here that which was the known cause of the poverty and disgrace of the great city of New York—no land where a groggery could stand. [Applause.] Twelve years have passed, and from that small beginning is formed a village made by enterprise and the railroad, and where there has never been one drop of liquor openly exposed for sale. Sir, we are prospered in that. God has been with us, and sent there noble men and nobler women. They have been with us in devotion from the beginning, and when I have seen them there, and witnessed their endurance—when I know how their hearts beat in sympathy with us, and that they are with us to-night—I am reminded of the highest compliment I ever heard, and it was by a son of the Emerald Isle, who, just landed, hearing an orator speak in most eloquent and glowing terms of woman, said to his friend, " O, Patrick, by my soul, if I had not been a man, would I not love to have been a woman!" The temperance people of Iowa have the co-operation of the ladies, to whom the eloquence of man can't do justice. The judicial district in which I reside, embracing one hundred thousand people, is comparatively free from intoxication. What are the results? Not a gateway there to the abodes of poverty and woe, and we may soon have State's prison room to let. We have already in our insane asylum taken in the unfortunate insane from Minnesota, and we may take in also some unfortunates from abroad. There are few in our jails and poor-houses, and I am informed by the judge of my district that he has not tried a man for murder during six years. It is a glorious fact, too, that when the year 1867 began, every State officer—aye, from governor down, including the supreme judges and the clerks, and all connected with the State departments—pledged themselves to one another, on their honor as gentlemen, that they would abide by the temperance pledge in not touching, tasting, or countenancing this poison. [Applause.]

I wish all our States may have such a record. I do not wish to boast of the Hawkeyes, but desire rather to give facts for your encouragement. Our colleges were never so flourishing; a greater number are found in the schools and churches; an increase of hundreds of thousands of acres of virgin soil are being turned over each year. We hope in this Congress there will be no efforts made for cheap whisky. The higher the better; better to have five and ten dollar whisky than anything lower for our rural population. We should see not how much duty can be got out of whisky, but, like Gladstone, England's financier, how little we should have, and how much duty can be got from that *little*. That is a temperance measure that will subserve morals everywhere. I have seen the effects of whisky. I have not the experience of a reformed drunkard, but I have marked its woes and desolations. It is a poison. There is a universal prescription in a new country based on the philosophy *similia similibus curantur*, and when a man is bitten by a rattlesnake or a copperhead, an application of whisky will save him—and the poorer whisky it is, the better for that purpose. There is no poison of the rattlesnake or the copperhead that can withstand this villainous compound; it drives it out. But there was a man harvesting who had been bitten in his finger, and his arm began to swell, and he inquired what should be done, and the first thing they brought him was whisky. He would not use it. They reasoned with him; his arm had swollen to his shoulder. They said: "You will die; take the whisky; don't be a fool." But said he: "Let the arm swell; let me die; I have been poisoned by whisky twenty years; I loathe it; and if I am to die, God helping me, I will die a sober man." [Applause.]

He desired to go to his Creator in his right mind. There was another remedy, and he was saved, and shall have historic rank with the noble Senator pledged from Illinois. Sir, the earth shook under that tread which has just destroyed the slavery of millions, and let this wide land,

without the clangor of arms, be blest by the emancipation
of other millions from the thralldom of the cup of intoxication. [Applause.]

ADDRESS OF HON. J. W. PATTERSON,

Of New Hampshire.

MR. PRESIDENT—I should hardly feel justified in detaining
this audience at so late an hour. Indeed, perhaps, I ought
not to speak on the subject of temperance at all, for I know
very well that people much prefer specimens from a ruined
city for essays on its fallen glories. I could but think that I
was of very little account in this temperance movement, while
listening to the eloquent words which have already been
spoken to this audience, for while the thoughts and actions
of others are inspired by the enthusiasm of a new birth in the
cause, I learned my temperance from a sainted mother in
childhood. The Senator who addressed us, said that the
inebriate who conquered his appetites did a nobler and a
grander work than the Spartan band at the Pass of Thermopylæ, and it occurred to me that these same Spartans
raised a stone lion there at the gates of Thermopylæ, that all
passers-by in the future might remember the heroic daring of
Leonidas and his three hundred. But I think we have raised
here a nobler monument than the Greeks raised at the gates
of Thermopylæ, for we place before you a Spartan himself:

> " And the elements
> So mix in him, that nature might stand up
> And say to all the world, this is a man."

I suppose it is not the purpose of the Society, in holding

these meetings and allowing ten-minute speeches, to discuss at length the principles that underlie the temperance cause, but simply to express to the great people whom we represent in the farthest extremity of the nation, our sympathy with the grand uprising which we see in every portion of the land—to show to them that their representatives are ready to co-operate with them in doing what may be done to save our people from the moral destruction which seems to overshadow the land. You know very well that the temperance cause has been somewhat interrupted for the last four or five years. While our young men, our able-bodied men, from every section and State of the nation have been battling to save the Union, and while thus engaged have been exposed to the dangers of the camp and the march, they have been almost necessitated to the use of intoxicating drinks as a support in the midst of their trials and hardships. As a consequence, appetites have been kindled in many of these brave fellows. It is not strange—it is a common, but fearful result of war.

They have now returned to their old homes and industries, and must be made to feel again the saving power of their influence. They are made of too good stuff to be lost to society and the great interests of the age. Men who had the moral power to stand and fight in the fire-sheeted field of Gettysburg, when grape and shrapnell rained upon them; who advanced the loyal banner along the fiery gauntlet with Sherman, till they planted it upon the defenses and churches of Atlanta, and viscounted the traitorous confederacy from the river to the sea; men who could cut that swath of death through the Wilderness, fighting a month of battles in as many days; who could fold their cordon of fire around the doomed capital of rebellion, and smother treason on the very birthplace of liberty, are too good for drunkards. [Applause.]

It is our purpose to save these defenders of liberty, as the
strength and beauty of this generation, and the glory of those
who shall come after them. We would save them to their
friends, their country, and the cause of civilization. I know
it is very common for men to say of those who are engaged
in this cause, that they are Utopian dreamers. Now, I remember, sir, in 1834, when James Buckingham brought into
the English Parliament a resolution for the appointment of a
committee to investigate the cause, extent, and evils of a too
free use of intoxicating drinks, that a sneer and a titter arose
in that assembly of English law-makers, and many members
left the room because they would not be annoyed with such
nonsense. But that great, honest, eloquent man brought to
bear upon them the evils which intemperance had inflicted
upon his country in such glowing terms, showed them so
clearly that a hundred millions of pounds sterling were annually lost to the nation by the use of intoxicating drinks;
showed them that sixty thousand of the best men of England
went to an untimely grave every year from its use; demon-
strated so impressively to them that what Sir Matthew Hale
said was true, that four-fifths of the criminals of the land were
made so by intoxicating drinks; that the noblest intellect and
the purest affections went down and became imbruted by its
use, that they who began with a titter ended with tears, and
the committee was appointed from the best men in Parliament, and one of the ablest reports ever made upon the
subject was made by them.

The evil has not been lessened in our day. We are sometimes told that we ought not to attempt to curtail the use of
whisky or intoxicating drinks, *because* a large portion of the
revenue of the country is raised from whisky; and, they say,
those men who are engaged in the business are among the
most *honorable men.* Honorable *men!* In the last year

they have cheated the Government out of fifty millions of revenue. When we should have had eighty millions, we have had less than thirty. They first cheated the Government out of this revenue, then they raised the price of the article as high as the increased tariff would allow, and so cheat the victims of their nefarious business both in their taxes and the indulgence of their appetites. Would it not be vastly better, both for the wealth and the morals of our people, if the raw products from which whisky is manufactured were used directly in commerce, or in some productive consumption? Men who would engage in this traffic are the allies of every crime and the enemies of every virtue. [Applause.] But I must not detain you. I shall only say this, that our object is to save the young men of the country—their bodies and their souls. It is a great and difficult work, for all the literature of the past has intrenched men in the use of wine and strong drink. Why, old Pindar sings its praises, and Horace has his

> " *Nunc est bibendum, nunc pede libero,*
> *Pulsanda tellus.*"

Genius and beauty, eloquence and art, have immortalized this shame of men. But we wish to turn away from this false basis, and commence a career more honorable and glorious to our people.

Others have enlarged upon the sorrows of domestic life, the sufferings of the innocent and the helpless, the burdens and deprivations of society which flow from this bitter source, but I urge now simply the lower consideration of physical preservation—a sound body as the essential of a sound mind. This strong and beautiful organism is the cunning workmanship of a Divine hand, and the channel through which invisible ideas and spiritual forces pass into the framework of nature and of history—the instrument by which mind and Deity work their miracles of art and civilization. To us is committed the responsibility of preserving and beautifying this temple of the invisible. Once given over to strong drink, and it becomes a ruin and a shame. The dissipations of a single winter demoralized and ruined a victorious army at Capua. In time, it will stamp feebleness and decay upon a whole people. Do nothing in this cause, and your five hundred thousand drunkards will be the progenitors of an enervated and besotted nation. This generation should not only give to the future its brilliant record, but a race of children who can advance upon the achievements of the fathers, and cause the glory of the past to dim in the splendor of their works. Not liberty only, but civilization and the Christian faith, are to be committed to the custody of our posterity.

How shall this great work be accomplished ? Ordinarily, men can not conquer appetites by force of will. To attempt to dash the cup from the lips by a volition is vain. You may as well attempt to hold the planets by threads of gossamer. The wild war-horses of passion will not be thus curbed and tamed. You must put upon them the rein of some force in the soul stronger than the appetite you would conquer. Pleasure will become as circumspect as a saint under the love of gain ; close-fisted avarice becomes prodigal when the love of power awakes in the soul; but ambition, avarice, pleasure, all passions become as submissive as children when the voice of God is heard in the heart calling us to the loftier duties of our Christian faith. Here is the secret of power, the shibboleth of success.

It is by inspiring our whole population with some higher motive than the gratification of sense, that we shall accomplish the work which we have set before us. The sentiments of men must be regenerated and concentrated upon the work.

The spirit of an age is the power which revolutionizes its customs and its institutions. This is that

> " Mystery in the soul of state
> Which hath an operation more divine
> Than our mere chroniclers dare meddle with."

We seek to save millions of young men who will command the labor and hundreds of millions of the productive capital of the country. It is that our country may not become poor and our future population enfeebled and miserable as the old Greeks and Romans did under the influence of luxury, and so give up their liberties and their greatness to some more virtuous but less cultivated people, that we devote ourselves to this work. It is the future, as well as the present, that we are battling for, and it is a noble cause—the most glorious that we can labor in—and they who sneer, and say we are fanatical and Quixotic, have not yet reached the conception of the highest good, and can not comprehend the great interests of their time. [Applause.]

After singing by the children, under the charge of Mr. VAN METER, of New York, the assembly was dismissed.

COMPARATIVE PHYSIOGNOMY—PORTRAITS OF A LION AND MAN.

"What They Say."—Notices of the Press.

Everybody is influenced in forming opinions by what others say. And it requires everybody to know everything and to do everything. A great book, like a great public work, is, or should be, the culmination of all past knowledge in that interest. Webster's Dictionary contains the gist of all preceding dictionaries. The electric telegraph was suggested centuries ago, and all mankind, dead and living, have contributed to its establishment. So the newspaper press throughout the world may be said to echo the voice of the people. The *Philadelphia Press* says:

Mr. Wells has put the thought, the practical experience, the close observation, and the professional collection of a life-time into this important physiological work. He treats, as Lavater did, of Physiognomy, shows its harmony with Phrenology, and explains, to elucidate both sciences, the whole structure of the human body. He treats of temperaments, and contrasts the separate features of various human races, showing also how character is affected by climate. Very curious, too, are his illustrations of comparative Physiognomy, showing the animal types of the human race. The price of the work is $5.

A familiar chapter on Phrenology is introduced, and then follows one on the anatomy of the face, with a close analysis of each feature. First, the chin. No one will dispute Mr. Wells as to the infinite variety of chins; but we are sure many will be startled to hear that this unpretending terminus of the face has been quietly telling their love secrets. The jaws and teeth also tell their own tales of character. "The closest mouth can hide no secrets from the physiognomist."—*The Anti-Slavery Standard.*

The treatise of Mr. Wells, which is admirably printed and profusely illustrated, is probably the most complete hand-book upon the subject in the language. It contains a synopsis of the history of Physiognomy, with notices of all the different systems which have been promulgated, and critical examinations of the eyes, the noses, the mouths, the ears, and the brows of many distinguished and notorious characters.—*New York Tribune.*

It contains a treatise on every feature and whatever indicates peculiarity of character, the knowledge of which requires appropriate education to bring into subjugation and be made to answer a good end, without which it would mar and injure the pleasures of life. All who can afford to possess this compendium will have value received for the expense.—*New York Christian Intelligencer.*

It is a digest of Ethnology, it gives us the symptomatology of insanity, it treats of Physiology and Hygiene, and, incidentally, of Zoology. The chapter on the grades of intelligence is instructive, and that on comparative Physiognomy is exceedingly entertaining.—*American Educational Monthly.*

There are very few men or women who do not, consciously or unconsciously, practice Physiognomy every day of their lives. They may ridicule the idea that the shape of a man's head, the configuration of his nose, or the appearance of his eyes, furnish any guide to an estimate of his character or disposition, and yet the man of business will refuse an applicant employment because his glance is restless and uneasy instead of firm and decided; and every lady will quietly but quickly form her judgment regarding the gentleman who may be presented to her at an evening party.—*New York Times.*

See What They Say!

THE PHRENOLOGICAL JOURNAL AND LIFE ILLUSTRATED is a handsome quarto, published monthly, devoted to the SCIENCE OF MAN, including PHRENOLOGY, PHYSIOLOGY, PHYSIOGNOMY, PSYCHOLOGY, ETHNOLOGY, SOCIOLOGY, etc. It is the only Journal of the kind in America, or, indeed, in the world. Terms only $3 a year in advance. Samples 30 cts. Address SAMUEL R. WELLS, 389 Broadway, New York.

EDITORIAL AND OTHER NOTICES.

Its typographical appearance is neat, and each number is profusely illustrated. This Magazine, now ably edited by Mr. S. R. Wells, has steadily grown in public favor, and its counsels on subjects pertaining to health, education and physical culture are sound, timely and emphatic. It was among the earliest journals in this country to discuss these subjects in a popular and convincing manner, and in addition to its speciality of Phrenology, it contains a great deal of curious and interesting matter.—*N. Y. Evening Post.*

Few books will better repay perusal in the family than this rich storehouse of instruction and entertainment, which never fails to illustrate the practical philosophy of life, with its lively expositions, appropriate anecdotes and agreeable sketches of distinguished individuals.—*N. Y. Tribune.*

It takes no longer to read this periodical than any other which comes to our office. Its articles are various and interesting, and beneficial to the intellect and morality of the readers.—*Religious Herald, Hartford.*

Perhaps no publication in the country is guided by clearer common sense or more self-reliant independence. Certainly none seem better designed to promote the health, happiness and usefulness of its readers; and, although we cannot imagine a person who could read a number of it without dissent from some of its opinions, we should be equally at a loss to fancy one who could do so without pleasure and profit.—*Round Table.*

Besides the matter pertaining to its speciality, it contains a great variety of articles that will interest many readers.—*Christian Intelligencer.*

One of the pleasantest and most readable papers that comes to our office. It is always filled with interesting valuable matter.—*N. Y. Chronicle.*

A periodical which, more, perhaps, than any other publication in the world, is calculated to do good to its readers—to promote their physical, moral and intellectual health—to point out the dangers and temptations of life, and indicate the remedy for any evils that may have already been entailed. Alive, progressive, shrewd, practical, fully up to, if not in advance of the times in every respect, this monthly is working incalculable good, exerting its influence even upon those unaware of its existence. It ought to have a place in every family, and once having gained a foothold, its maintenance of it is sure.—*Trenton Monitor.*

Many of the practical teachings of the JOURNAL are of the highest value in the promotion of physical development and health, and *all aim at moral improvement.*—*The Methodist.*

The PHRENOLOGICAL JOURNAL is indispensable to believers in the science, and valuable and illustrative to the general reader. It is edited with marked ability, and beautifully printed.—*Christian Inquirer.*

We find both instruction and amusement in this monthly visitor.—*Christian Advocate Journal.*

There are few periodicals more truly valuable as household companions than this publication. We always find it readable throughout, and always up to a high standard of instructive family literature. The specialties are health and education, and on these topics its editorials and selections are unrivalled.—*Wheeling Intelligencer.*

FROM A LADY.

S. R. WELLS,—Dear Sir,—I cannot let this opportunity pass without telling you the incalculable benefits I have derived from the study of your publications. I have been a constant reader of them for eighteen years. My mother (God bless her) commenced taking LIFE ILLUSTRATED, with its first issue, and the PHRENOLOGICAL JOURNAL for the benefit of her only son (then a small boy), and her daughters. I firmly believe those works have contributed more toward making us true men and women than any others excepting the Bible. My brother still takes the A. P. J., and doubtless will always do so. For twelve years I labored as a school teacher, until worn out nature compelled me to rest. Part of that time I used *Life Illustrated* in my school, deriving great benefit to my pupils and myself therefrom. I have been married two and a half years, and housekeeping nearly a year, and I esteem my Journal the finest book I can have upon my table. Some have called it my "Bible." They were mistaken only in one point. It stands just *after* my Bible, for it helps me to *better understand* that book of all books. I cannot live and keep house contentedly without it, and you may place my name upon your list of "Life Subscribers."

I sometimes feel impelled to write—impelled by some invisible power to write my "Best Thoughts" for the benefit of others, and then I mind me of those laboring toward the same great end, who are far more gifted than myself, and thinking my efforts might be fruitless, I remain a silent but hopeful spectator. Did my family carve permit. I would gladly labor for the spread of the Journal. As it is, I can only advocate it, or use my woman's prerogative—*talk* it to all my friends. The Journal is not a more welcome visitor to any of us than to my baby boy (1¾ years old), who hails its coming with shouts, and will sit an hour turning the pages and examining the faces as carefully as many a "child of an older growth."

Pardon my intruding upon your precious time with so long a letter, my heart was full and I could not help it. Gratefully and respectfully, Mrs. ——.

I can not do without your excellent *Journal.* It is indispensable to those in the ranks of the Christian ministry. REV. S. M.

I would not lose the *Journal* for $10 a year.—J. E. B.

As a family, we all feel that we cannot give up the A. P. J., for its pleasant face and interesting converse serves to brighten and make more *warm and genial* our happy fireside. It helps attract our dear boys to their home these long winter evenings, and keeps them away from public places of evil influences, therefore send it by all means to Mrs. H. J. S.

I would be unwilling to exchange it for any periodical I know of.—A H. A.

Were it four dollars a year instead of three, I could withdraw my name from your list of subscribers. M. Z. C.

I do not know how I can possibly get along without it.—G. R. H.

Your *Journal* is appreciated, not only by us, but by our neighbors who have read and re-read them until the numbers are quite worn.—E. U.

THE
Phrenological Journal
AND
LIFE ILLUSTRATED.
FOR 1867

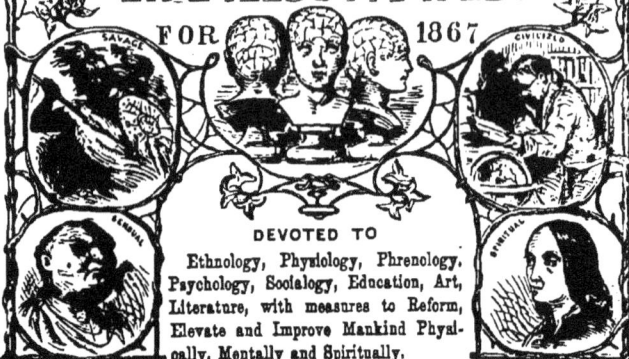

DEVOTED TO

Ethnology, Physiology, Phrenology, Psychology, Sociology, Education, Art, Literature, with measures to Reform, Elevate and Improve Mankind Physically, Mentally and Spiritually.

S. R. WELLS, Editor.

The Study and Improvement of Man in all his Relations is our object.

The Natural History of Man —including the Manners, Customs, Religions and Modes of Life in different Families, Tribes and Nations will be given.

Physiology, the Laws of Life and Health, including Dietetics, Exercise, Sleep, Study, Bodily Growth, etc., will be presented on strictly Hygienic principles.

Phrenology.—The Brain and its Functions, the Temperaments, Location of the Organs, Choice of Pursuits, etc., given.

Physiognomy; or, "The Human Face Divine," with "Signs of Character, and How to Read Them" scientifically.

The Human Soul—Psychology.—Its Nature, Office and Condition in Life and Death; Man's Spiritual State in the Here and in the Hereafter. Very interesting.

Biography.—In connection with, Portraits and Practical Delineations of Character of our most distinguished men.

Marriage forms a part of the life of every well organized human being. The elements of love are inborn. The objects of Marriage stated. All young people require instruction and direction in the selection of suitable life-companions. Phrenology throws light on the subject. Let us consult it.

The Choice of Pursuits.—How to select a pursuit to which a person is best adapted : Law, Medicine, Divinity, Invention ; Mechanics ; Agriculture ; Manufacturing ; Commerce, etc. "Let us put the right man in the right place."

Miscellaneous. — Churches, Schools, Prisons, Asylums, Hospitals, Reformatories, etc., described with Modes of Worship, Education, Training, and Treatment, given in the new vol. of THE PHRENOLOGICAL JOURNAL AND LIFE ILLUSTRATED.

Terms.—A New Volume, the 46th, commences with the July Number. Published monthly, in quarto forms, at $3 a year in advance. Sample numbers sent by first post, 30 cents. Clubs of Ten or more, $2.00 each per copy. Subscribe now.

PLEASE ADDRESS
SAMUEL R. WELLS,
NO. 389 BROADWAY,
NEW YORK, U. S. A.

www.ingramcontent.com/pod-product-compliance
Lightning Source LLC
Chambersburg PA
CBHW031816090426
42739CB00008B/1302